The MAILBOX®
The Education Center®

Grades 1–3

Daily Journal Prompts

Two journal prompts for every day of the year!

- **730 Holiday, Seasonal, and General Prompts for August–July**

- **Reproducible Journal Covers**

- **Reproducible Student Writing Sheet**

Managing Editor: Debra Liverman

Editorial Team: Becky S. Andrews, Kimberley Bruck, Karen P. Shelton, Diane Badden, Thad H. McLaurin, Debra Liverman, Lauren E. Cox, Peggy W. Hambright, Karen A. Brudnak, Sarah Hamblet, Hope Rodgers, Dorothy C. McKinney, Amy Barsanti, Denine Carter, Stacie Stone Davis, Laura Wagner

Production Team: Lisa K. Pitts, Pam Crane, Rebecca Saunders, Jennifer Tipton Cappoen, Chris Curry, Sarah Foreman, Theresa Lewis Goode, Ivy L. Koonce, Clint Moore, Greg D. Rieves, Barry Slate, Donna K. Teal, Tazmen Carlisle, Amy Kirtley-Hill, Kristy Parton, Debbie Shoffner, Cathy Edwards Simrell, Lynette Dickerson, Mark Rainey

www.themailbox.com

W9-AVL-414

Table of Contents

Manufactured in the United States
10 9 8 7 6 5 4 3

How to Use This Book

Make Monthly Journal Response Booklets

At the beginning of each month, make one copy of the appropriate monthly cover (see pages 100–111) for each student. Then make several copies of the lined writing page (see page 112) for each student. Stack the lined sheets of paper, place the monthly cover on top, and then staple along the left-hand side to create a booklet. Have each student decorate the cover with markers or crayons.

Use for Guided Daily Journal Writing

At the start of each day, select one of the two prompts to write on the board, or write both prompts on the board and instruct each student to select the one that interests her the most. (If you have access to an overhead projector, a transparency of the prompts will be a timesaver and can be reused year after year.) Have students write their journal entries in their monthly journal response booklets. If desired, discuss the daily writing topic with students before they begin writing.

Use for Independent Journal Writing

Post copies of a month's worth of journal prompts in a center or on a classroom bulletin board. Every day, challenge each child to select one prompt from the appropriate day to respond to in her monthly journal response booklet.

AUGUST

August 1

✏ Describe your perfect day. What would you do? Who would you see?

✏ August is National Inventor's Month! Imagine that you have just invented a bubble solution that makes incredibly long lasting bubbles. Write an advertisement convincing others to buy it.

August 2

✏ Think about your favorite summertime activity. Describe it and tell why it is your favorite.

✏ Imagine you are going to a cookout and can bring anyone you want. Who would be your perfect guest? Why?

August 3

✏ On August 3, 1492, Christopher Columbus set sail on his journey that led to his discovery of the New World. Write about a time that you tried something for the first time. Explain how you felt.

✏ Imagine you could compete in any Olympic event. Which event would you enter and why?

August 4

✏ Would you rather spend the day at your friend's house or have your friend spend the day at your house? Explain.

✏ Imagine that all the animals in the ocean can talk. Write about a conversation you overhear two animals having.

August 5

✏ Name three or more reasons why everyone should learn how to swim.

✏ Describe the perfect summer picnic. Where is it? What foods are in the basket?

August 6

✏ If you could ride a wave to any place in the world, where would you go? What would you do there?

✏ Imagine that you could spend a day underwater. Write about your adventures.

August 7

✏ National Mustard day is celebrated the first Saturday in August. Write about a pretend conversation between a mustard bottle and a ketchup bottle.

✏ Name one drink that tastes better with ice and one drink that tastes better without ice. Explain why.

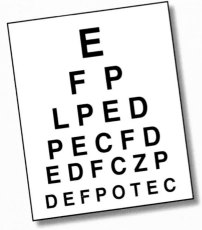

August 8

✏ August is Children's Eye Health and Safety Month. Describe three or more things you can do to take good care of your eyes.

✏ Explain how your day would be different if you could see only in black and white.

August 9

✎ Name three ways that a beach and a desert are alike. Name three ways that they are different.

✎ What zoo animal are you most like? Explain why you think this is so.

August 10

✎ The Smithsonian Institution, a collection of museums and research centers in Washington, DC, was founded in 1846. Have you visited a museum? What did you learn there?

✎ Would you rather visit an art museum, a history museum, or a science museum? Explain.

August 11

✎ Joanna Coles, creator of the Magic School Bus series, was born on August 11. If you could take a magic school bus ride anywhere, where would you go? What would you do there?

✎ Would you rather be a crab or a seagull? Why?

August 12

✎ The home sewing machine was invented by Isaac Singer on August 12, 1851. Other than clothing, list as many items as you can that are sewn.

✎ IBM introduced the first personal computer, or PC, on August 12, 1981. Imagine an alien is visiting Earth. Describe what a personal computer is and what it is used for.

August 13

✎ Would you rather spend your vacation in the mountains or at the beach? Explain.

✎ Imagine that you found a magic shell on the beach. Describe its magical powers and tell how you would use them.

August 14

✎ National Garage Sale Day is held the second Saturday in August. A garage sale is a sale of personal items out of a person's garage or out in front of his or her home. List five items from your bedroom that you would sell at a garage sale. Explain why you chose each item.

✎ Would you rather be too hot or too cold? Why?

August 15

✎ August 15 is National Relaxation Day. Describe your most relaxing day.

✎ Create a new game that can be played using a ball and a jump rope. Describe the game.

August 16

✎ Imagine that you are a miner who just found gold. Write a letter to your parents telling them all about it.

✎ Would you rather have a swimming pool at your house or live in a house near the ocean? Explain.

AUGUST

August 17

✎ Imagine that sand could be used in place of gasoline for running a car's engine. How might this affect the environment?

✎ Make up a story that explains why crabs walk sideways.

August 18

✎ Name five or more things that you can do during a long car ride to help time pass more quickly.

✎ Describe why someone might want to use an umbrella at the beach. How does this compare to someone using an umbrella when it rains?

August 19

✎ National Aviation Day is August 19. Imagine that you are Orville Wright landing after your first successful flight. Write a letter convincing a guest to join you on a future flight.

✎ Would you rather be an airplane or a boat? Why?

August 20

✎ What is your favorite color? List ten objects that are that color.

✎ If you could be an ocean animal, which one would you be? Why?

August 21

✏ Poet's Day is August 21. Write a poem about a friend.

✏ Explain how to ride a bicycle.

August 22

✏ August 22 is National Punctuation Day. Explain why punctuation is important.

✏ Imagine you are a melting ice pop. Describe how you feel.

August 23

✏ If you were a fish, would you rather live in a lake, a river, an ocean, or a fish tank? Explain.

✏ Imagine that you found a stray kitten. Describe how you would attempt to find its owner.

August 24

✏ What four sounds remind you of summer? Why?

✏ Imagine you are a bumblebee for a day. Where would you fly? What would you do?

A U G U S T

August 25

 What one item would you want with you while at summer camp? Explain.

✎ Would you rather ride in a motorboat or a sailboat? Explain.

August 26

✎ Pretend that whatever you draw with sidewalk chalk becomes real. What three things will you draw? Why?

✎ Create a new flavor of ice cream. Describe what it is and how it tastes.

August 27

 Write five tips for creating a successful lemonade stand.

✎ Imagine that a neighbor asked you to walk her dog every day during the summer. Would you do it? Explain.

August 28

✎ Pretend one hour is being added to each day. What one thing would you choose to do during the extra hour? Why?

 Write a letter convincing your parent to allow your best friend to join you on your family vacation.

August 29

✎ Do you prefer to eat ice cream in a cone or in a dish? Explain.

✎ Write three or more reasons why a person might want to ice-skate in the summer.

August 30

✎ Describe your perfect school lunch. How often would you like to eat this lunch?

✎ Think of one goal you want to accomplish this school year. Describe how you plan to reach your goal.

August 31

✎ Would you rather have P.E. as your first class of the day or as your last class of the day? Why?

✎ Describe three or more ways to use math when you are not at school.

AUGUST

September 1

✎ September is National Very Important Parents (VIP) Month. Describe three or more qualities that are important for a good parent to have.

✎ Write a story explaining why many owls make the "whoo" sound.

Whoo!

September 2

✎ National Waffle Week is celebrated the first full week in September. Describe the toppings you'd add to make the perfect waffle for breakfast.

✎ Think about what you ate for breakfast this morning. Was this a healthy choice? Explain.

September 3

✎ Backpack Safety America Month is celebrated in September to remind students, parents, and teachers about the importance of safely packing and carrying a backpack. Write a letter to your school's principal convincing her to recognize this special month at your school.

✎ Name three or more things that you like to always carry in your backpack. Explain.

September 4

I wish...

✎ Imagine that you could snap your fingers and wish for something to help someone other than yourself. Name whom you would help and describe your wish.

✎ If you could change one thing about the first day of school this year, what would it be? Explain.

September 5

✎ Labor Day is celebrated the first Monday in September. Do you think a garbage truck driver, a doctor, and a professional football player all have important jobs? Explain.

✎ Pretend you are a squirrel hiding acorns on the school playground. Where would you hide your stash? Explain.

September 6

✎ Describe the best sound to wake up to in the morning.

✎ Imagine that you are having trouble sleeping. Describe what you would do to help send yourself into dreamland.

September 7

✎ September is Children's Good Manners Month. Describe how to use good manners when answering the telephone.

✎ What three manners would you like to see required of all students while in the school cafeteria? Explain.

September 8

✎ Jack Prelutsky, author of *It's Raining Pigs & Noodles*, was born on September 8. Imagine that you just stepped outside, and it is raining strange objects. Write about what you see.

✎ What subject do you enjoy least in school? Explain how you would change it to make it more enjoyable.

September 9

✏️ September is National Honey Month. List ten or more words about honey. Write a poem about honey using as many of your words as possible.

✏️ Would you rather be a bee or an ant? Explain.

September 10

✏️ Substitute Teacher Appreciation Week is held the second full week in September. List five or more things that you can do to make the school day easier for a substitute teacher.

✏️ Pretend that you could send a substitute student to go to school for you when you are out sick. Who would you send? Explain.

September 11

✏️ Would you rather explore a cave or climb a mountain? Explain.

✏️ Write a letter to your teacher convincing her to let you eat lunch outside today. Give at least three reasons why you think this is a good idea.

September 12

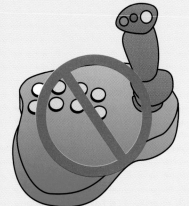

✏️ Video Games Day is September 12. Imagine that all video games were banned. Would you be happy or unhappy? Explain.

✏️ National Grandparents Day is celebrated in September. List three questions that you would like to ask an elderly person about life when they were your age.

September 13

✎ Would you rather have your own birthday party or go to someone else's party? Explain.

✎ Author Roald Dahl was born on September 13. In his book *James and the Giant Peach*, James rolls away in a giant peach that grew from magic crystals. Imagine you could travel in a giant piece of fruit. What type of fruit would you choose? Explain.

September 14

✎ September 14 is the anniversary of the start of the first solo balloon flight across the Atlantic Ocean. Imagine you are preparing to spend five days in a balloon. What three items would you pack for your trip?

✎ Would you rather be able to run very fast or jump very high? Explain.

September 15

✎ Imagine that you have a new student in your class. Write directions telling her how to get to the library from your classroom.

✎ Do you prefer stories that are real or make-believe? Explain.

September 16

✎ On September 16, 1620, the Pilgrims set sail aboard the *Mayflower*. They landed in Plymouth, Massachusetts, on December 26. Imagine that you spent three months on a ship like the *Mayflower*. List five or more words to describe your trip.

✎ Do you prefer to work on school projects alone or with a group? Explain.

September 17

✎ Describe your favorite recess game for a rainy day.

✎ Pretend that you are an apple on a tree. Write about what you would say to a farmer to convince him to pick you.

September 18

✎ Think about your bedroom. Describe one thing you would add to your room to make it better.

✎ Would you rather hear a great story read aloud or watch the same story as a movie? Explain.

September 19

✎ How is a radio similar to a newspaper? Explain.

✎ Imagine that you are the teacher. What subject would you like to teach? Explain.

September 20

✎ Write five or more clues to describe a classroom item.

✎ Describe an outrageous fall hat. What features does it have that represent the fall season?

September 21

✎ Imagine that you are the teacher. Explain what you would do to get students to do their homework.

✎ If you were an animal, would you rather sleep during the day or during the night? Explain.

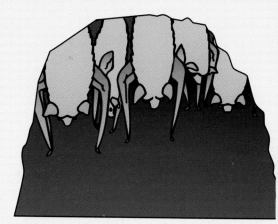

September 22

✎ September 22 is Elephant Appreciation Day. Imagine that you had a trunk like an elephant. How would your day be different?

✎ Are you more like a tree in the fall or a tree in the summer? Explain.

September 23

✎ Imagine that your best friend can't play with you today. Describe a favorite game that you could play by yourself.

✎ How are a backpack and a school bus alike? Explain.

September 24

✎ Do you prefer to color with markers or crayons? Explain.

✎ Pretend that you could buy one item today, but then you had to give it away to a friend tomorrow. What would you buy? Explain.

S
E
P
T
E
M
B
E
R

September 25

✎ National Dog Week is celebrated the last full week in September. Describe an unusual trick that you would teach a pet dog.

✎ Everyone should have a dog. Do you agree or disagree with this statement? Explain.

September 26

✎ September 26 is Johnny Appleseed's birthdate. Write a story about an imaginary character named Joann Flowerbud.

✎ Would you rather eat a fresh apple, some applesauce, or a slice of apple pie? Explain.

September 27

✎ Describe your favorite fall activity.

✎ Imagine that you just scored the winning touchdown in a football game. List five or more words to describe how you feel.

September 28

✎ Which school rule do you think is the most important? Explain.

✎ Think about your favorite cartoon character and your favorite book character. In what ways are they the same? In what ways are they different?

September 29

✎ Name three or more things that you can do that will make it easier for the janitor to clean your classroom.

✎ Do you prefer mornings, afternoons, or evenings? Explain.

September 30

✎ In what ways are getting ready for school and getting ready for work alike? In what ways are they different?

✎ Imagine that you are a tree whose leaves are beginning to change colors and will soon fall off. Describe how you feel.

October 1

✏️ October is National Roller Skating Month. Explain how school would be different if all students and teachers wore roller skates.

✏️ Would you rather live on a farm or in the city? Explain.

October 2

✏️ October is National Go on a Field Trip Month. Describe the perfect school field trip.

✏️ Pretend your class went on a field trip to an underwater castle. Describe the souvenir that you took home.

October 3

✏️ World Smile Day is held on the first Friday in October. What could you do for your best friend to make him or her smile?

✏️ Describe the funniest thing you have seen or heard this week.

October 4

✏️ The first Monday in October is Child Health Day. List three ways to keep your body healthy. Explain why each is important.

✏️ Imagine that you just raked a huge pile of fall leaves. Describe what you see, hear, and feel as you jump into the pile.

October 5

✎ World Teachers' Day is celebrated on October 5. Write a letter to one of your favorite teachers thanking him or her for being your teacher.

✎ Would you like to be a teacher when you grow up? Explain why or why not.

October 6

✎ The first full week in October is National Newspaper Week. Write a make-believe newspaper article that starts with "You are not going to believe this!"

✎ Pretend that an alien has just landed. What would you say to convince him to come to your school for show-and-tell?

October 7

✎ October is National Popcorn Poppin' Month. Make up a silly story explaining why popcorn pops.

✎ Pretend that you are the assistant in a scientist's lab. The room is filled with bottles, jars, liquids, and unknown objects. Describe what happens on your first day in the lab.

October 8

✎ World Egg Day is the second Friday in October. Are you more like a scrambled egg or a hard-boiled egg? Explain.

✎ What do you like most about October? Explain.

October 9

✎ Fire Prevention Week is the first or second week in October. Imagine that you were selected to spend a day at the fire department. What one thing would you like to do that day? Why?

✎ Imagine that you have been shrunk to the size of a crayon. Describe a typical day in your life.

October 10

✎ Imagine that you are walking through a pumpkin patch and you find a hidden door. Write a story about what happens when you open the door.

✎ What three words describe you right now? Explain why you chose each word.

October 11

✎ Columbus Day is celebrated on the second Monday in October. Imagine that Columbus's ship was actually a time machine and he landed in the New World in the current year. Write three or more things that might surprise him.

✎ What one food would you like to never eat again? Explain.

October 12

✎ Pretend that you are a scarecrow. What would you say to convince the farmer to take you down off the stick?

✎ Describe something that you do very well.

O C T O B E R

October 13

✏️ The week starting with the second Sunday in October is National School Lunch Week. Imagine that your principal wants to replace your school cafeteria with a fast-food restaurant. Explain why you think this is a good idea or a bad idea.

✏️ What kind of cereal are you most like? Explain.

October 14

✏️ List five or more things that are orange. Write a poem about the color orange.

✏️ Describe a Halloween costume that you can make using a laundry basket, a shoebox, and a black cape.

October 15

✏️ National Grouch Day is October 15. Describe something that makes you grouchy.

✏️ "Money doesn't grow on trees" is a popular saying. Explain what you think this means. What if money did grow on trees?

October 16

✏️ October 16 is Dictionary Day in honor of Noah Webster, who was born on this day. Other than looking up the meaning of a word, how else can you use a dictionary?

✏️ The third Saturday in October is Sweetest Day. This day was started many years ago when a worker at a candy company gave candy to the sick, shut-ins, and orphans. Describe what someone could do for you that would make you say, "Oh, that is so sweet!"

October 17

✏ October is National Cookie Month. Think about the ingredients that would go into your perfect cookie. Describe how your perfect cookie looks and tastes.

✏ In some parts of the country, cooler October air means it's time to wear sweatshirts and sweaters. Do you prefer wearing cooler-weather clothes or warmer-weather clothes? Explain.

October 18

✏ October is National Dental Hygiene Month. Imagine that your new monster friend has terrible teeth. Write him directions on how to properly care for them.

✏ What two items that you own are most special to you? What makes each item so special?

October 19

✏ Pretend that you are riding a bicycle that can suddenly fly. Describe what you see as you ride high above your neighborhood.

✏ Would you rather be a spider or a bat? Explain.

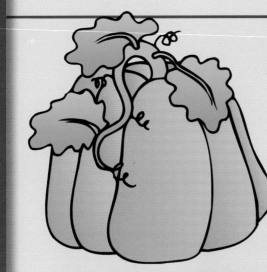

October 20

✏ Imagine that there is a Monster Ball being held tonight. Describe what this party might be like. What food would be served? What games would be played?

✏ List as many words as you can think of about pumpkins. Write a paragraph about pumpkins.

October 21

✎ List three or more characteristics of a good pet owner. Explain why each is important.

✎ Write a story about one night with your friends that starts with "It was a full moon…"

October 22

✎ October is Vegetarian Month. People who are vegetarians do not eat meat. What do you think would be the hardest part about being a vegetarian? Explain.

✎ A bat is the only mammal that can fly. If you could pick another animal and give it the ability to fly, which animal would you choose? Explain.

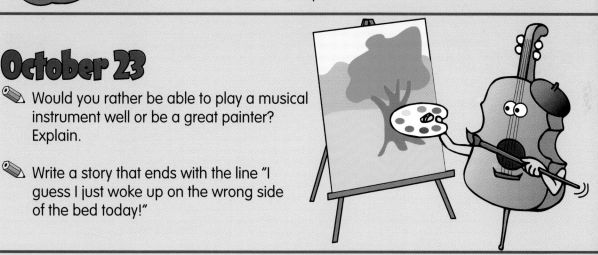

October 23

✎ Would you rather be able to play a musical instrument well or be a great painter? Explain.

✎ Write a story that ends with the line "I guess I just woke up on the wrong side of the bed today!"

School

First-Class Mail

October 24

✎ October is National Stamp Collecting Month. Describe a design for a postage stamp that would represent your school.

✎ If you were to start collecting something as a hobby, what would you collect? Explain why you chose this item.

October 25

✏️ Would you rather lengthen the school day by two hours and never have homework again or keep the day the same length and have homework every night? Explain.

✏️ Other than orange and black, what two colors do you think of when you think about fall? Explain.

October 26

✏️ Author and illustrator Steven Kellogg celebrates his birthday today. Would you rather write a book or draw the pictures for a book? Explain.

✏️ Pretend that your principal announced that tomorrow will be Bring Your Pet to School Day. Describe what you think school would be like.

October 27

✏️ Do you think that it would be a good idea for every student to have a computer at his desk in school? Explain.

✏️ Imagine that once you put on your Halloween costume, you would actually become that person or object for a day. What costume would you choose? Why?

October 28

✏️ Would you rather have cake or ice cream for your birthday? Explain.

✏️ If you could invite one person to come to your classroom for the day, who would it be? Why would you pick this person?

October 29

✎ During fall, some animals gather and store food for the winter. If you had to do this, what types of food would be in your stash?

✎ If you could build a robot to help you do one thing, what would it be? Explain.

October 30

✎ Describe a healthy meal that your entire family would enjoy. Don't forget dessert!

✎ Do you prefer wearing scary, funny, or beautiful Halloween costumes? Explain.

October 31

✎ Imagine that trick-or-treating has been canceled in your town. Explain what else you and your friends can do to celebrate Halloween.

✎ How are Halloween and Valentine's Day similar? How are they different?

November 1

✎ Today is National Family Literacy Day. What one book would you like to share with your family? Explain why you chose this book.

✎ November 1 is National Authors' Day. If you could ask the author of your favorite book two or more questions, what would they be?

November 2

✎ Imagine that you are working at the circus. Would you rather be an animal trainer, a clown, or a trapeze artist? Explain.

✎ As cold weather approaches, some animals begin to hibernate. Describe the perfect pajamas to wear if you had to hibernate all winter.

November 3

✎ November 3 is Sandwich Day. Pretend that you had to eat the same type of sandwich every day for a month. Describe what your sandwich would look and taste like.

✎ Compare a football field to your school playground. How are they alike? How are they different?

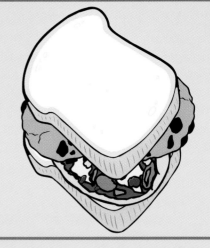

November 4

✎ November is Peanut Butter Lovers' Month. Are you a peanut butter lover? Explain why or why not.

✎ If you could change your name, would you? If so, what name would you select and why? If not, explain why you would keep your name.

PEANUT BUTTER

November 5

✎ Would you rather be the president of the United States or a movie star? Explain.

✎ Imagine that you are playing in the sand and you find a tunnel. Describe what happens next.

November 6

✎ November is Aviation History Month. Would you rather fly in a helicopter or in an airplane? Explain.

✎ If you lived on a farm, what crops would you grow? Explain.

November 7

✎ Rules are everywhere! Explain what a game of football would be like if there were no game rules to follow.

✎ Imagine that all students could choose which school they wanted to attend. Write three or more reasons why a student should choose to attend your school.

November 8

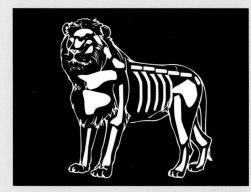

✎ The X ray was invented on this day in 1895. What object would you like to see the inside of if you could X-ray it? Explain.

✎ Imagine that you could see through walls. Do you think this would be a good thing or a bad thing? Explain.

November 9

✎ National Young Reader's Day is an annual November event. Do you prefer reading a book by yourself or having someone read to you? Explain.

✎ When the weather gets cold, some birds fly south to warmer weather. Imagine that you had to leave home for several months. What five items would you bring along other than your clothing?

I am so thankful...

November 10

✎ Complete five or more sentences that start with the words "I am so thankful…"

✎ Explain how school would be different if you did not use books or paper.

November 11

✎ November 11 is Veteran's Day. This day honors the men and women who have served in the United States armed forces. Do you think you would like to serve in the military one day? Explain.

✎ Describe what you think it would be like to be aboard a submarine ship.

SKATEBOARDING

November 12

✎ Imagine that you could create a class at school to learn about a topic of your choice. What topic would you choose? Explain.

✎ Describe your typical morning before school starts.

November 13

✎ World Kindness Day is celebrated on November 13. Write about a time when someone was very kind to you.

✎ Would you rather learn how to play the drums or the guitar? Explain.

November 14

✎ Today is National American Teddy Bear Day. Imagine that your teddy bear came to life. Write about one day that you spent with your furry friend.

✎ Think about a time when you were feeling sad. Explain what you did to make yourself feel better.

November 15

✎ November 15 is America Recycles Day. Do you think recycling is important? Explain.

✎ List as many uses as you can for an old newspaper.

November 16

✎ Children's Book Week is celebrated each November. Describe your favorite reading spot.

✎ Imagine that you are a farmer and it has not rained for weeks. Write a simple song or chant encouraging the rain to fall.

November 17

✎ November 17 is Homemade Bread Day. Describe your favorite way to eat bread.

✎ Imagine that you are stuck inside on a stormy day. Would you rather watch televison, play a game, or read a book? Explain.

YOU'RE INVITED TO A PARTY!

November 18

✎ Today is Mickey Mouse's Birthday. Tell how you would plan a party for him. Think about whom you would invite, how you would decorate, where you would have the party, what food you would serve, and what games you would play.

✎ Great American Smokeout is held in November to celebrate smoke-free environments. Write a letter to a friend telling why he should never try smoking.

November 19

✎ Olympic gold medal sprinter Gail Devers was born on this day in 1966. Describe how you would feel if you won an Olympic gold medal.

✎ Imagine that it just snowed for the first time this season. Describe three or more things that you'd like to do outside.

My name is Tag.

November 20

✎ November 20 is Name Your PC Day. What name would you give your computer? Explain.

✎ Would you rather be a houseplant or a plant out in the garden? Explain.

November 21

✎ Pumpkin Pie Day is November 21. This pie is a traditional Thanksgiving dessert. If you could change this, what dessert would you put in its place? Explain.

✎ November 21 is World Hello Day. Not everyone in the world speaks the same language. Create a new way of saying hello without speaking or waving your hand. Describe how to do it and why you chose this method.

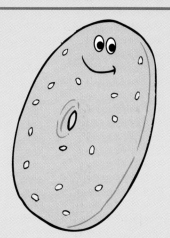

November 22

✎ Write a silly story explaining how bagels came to have holes in the middle.

✎ Would you rather be a turkey or a chicken? Explain.

November 23

✎ Imagine that you are a crow watching the very first Thanksgiving meal. Describe what you see and hear.

✎ In what ways do you think your family relies on you? Explain.

November 24

✎ The day before Thanksgiving is What Do You Love About America Day. Imagine that your parents want to move to another country. Write three or more reasons to convince them why you should stay in America.

✎ Would you rather be a fireman or a policeman? Explain.

N
O
V
E
M
B
E
R

November 25

✎ Marc Brown, author of the Arthur Adventure Series, was born on November 25. Some books in his series are *Arthur's First Sleepover*, *Arthur Goes to Camp*, and *Arthur Goes to School*. Imagine that Marc Brown asked you to come up with a new title for an Arthur Adventure book. Write the title and explain what will happen in the story.

✎ Thanksgiving is the last Thursday in November. Explain how you will celebrate Thanksgiving this year.

November 26

✎ November 26 is the birthday of Charles Schultz. He created the *Peanuts* comic strip. Would you rather be Charlie Brown or Snoopy? Explain.

✎ National Game and Puzzle week is held during the week of Thanksgiving. Do you prefer games or puzzles? Explain.

November 27

✎ Compare a fall night to a summer night.

✎ Imagine that you had to eat the same food every day for one week. Would you rather eat peanut butter and jelly sandwiches or pizza? Explain.

November 28

✎ Would you rather be a polar bear or a grizzly bear? Explain.

✎ By now, most stores and many homes have their Christmas decorations displayed. Do you think it is too early to decorate for Christmas? Explain.

November 29

✎ November 29 is Electronic Greetings Day. Which would you rather receive from a friend, a written letter or an email? Explain.

✎ Imagine that you could choose anyone in the world to be your pen pal. Who would you choose? Explain.

November 30

✎ Write a poem titled "Goodbye, November. Hello, December."

✎ Would you rather have wings or fins? Explain.

December 1

✏️ Jan Brett, author of *Armadillo Rodeo,* was born on December 1. In this story, an armadillo follows a red boot worn by a girl. Imagine that you followed a boot around. Describe three places the boot might go.

✏️ On December 1, 1891, James Naismith, a P.E. teacher, created the game of basketball. He nailed peach baskets to opposite ends of a gym and gave students soccer balls to throw into them. What do you think makes a basketball better than a soccer ball for playing the game of basketball? Explain.

December 2

✏️ Cookie Cutter Week is celebrated during the first week of December. If you had to bake a cookie in a shape that would tell something about yourself, what shape would you choose? Explain.

✏️ Describe your favorite smells during the holiday season.

December 3

✏️ Do you prefer to wear mittens or gloves? Explain.

✏️ In what ways are boots and scarves alike? In what ways are they different?

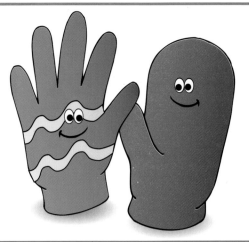

B	I	N	G	O
3	29	41	61	82
6	34	44	62	84
11	37	FREE	65	89
17	39	55	71	90
20	40	57	72	91

December 4

✏️ December is Bingo's Birthday Month. Do you think bingo is a fair game? Explain.

✏️ Pretend that you are keeping a wonderful secret. What is the secret? When the time is right, who will be the first person that you tell and why?

December 5

✏️ Imagine that you spend all morning building a snowpal, and then the weather suddenly turns warm. What can you do to try to keep your snowpal frozen for another day?

✏️ Describe the best gingerbread house that you could make.

December 6

✏️ Candy canes are a popular Christmas candy. Describe your favorite holiday treat.

✏️ What do you like most about cold weather? What do you like least?

December 7

✏️ Imagine that you are a snowball flying through the air. What are you thinking?

✏️ What is your favorite section of the library? Explain.

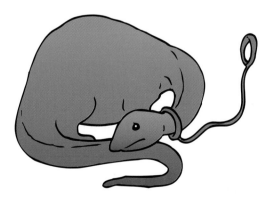

December 8

✏️ Would you like to have a dinosaur for a pet? Explain why or why not.

✏️ What toy could be placed in a cereal box that would make you want to buy that cereal? Explain.

December 9

✎ Latkes, or potato pancakes, are a special Hanukkah treat. Describe your favorite food that is eaten during the holiday season.

✎ Describe your kindergarten classroom as you remember it.

December 10

✎ List four or more words that rhyme with the word *snow*. Then write a poem about snow.

✎ Imagine that you are flying aboard a giant candy cane. Describe where you are going.

December 11

✎ Imagine that you just finished building a gingerbread house and suddenly a light comes on inside the house. Write a story about what happens next.

✎ Write a letter to your school's principal convincing her or him to make your school week only four days long. Give at least three reasons in your letter.

December 12

✎ Poinsettia Day is recognized on December 12. What silly things can you do to help a poinsettia feel special on this day?

✎ Imagine that you could own your own store. What kind of store would it be? Explain.

December 13

 Imagine that as you are falling asleep, a reindeer flies past your window and motions for you to follow. Write about what happens next.

 What would you do if you saw a classmate being treated unfairly on the playground? Why?

December 14

 Many gifts are given during the month of December. Make a list of gifts that you can give your family and friends without spending any money.

 Would you rather be a polar bear or a penguin? Explain.

December 15

 Imagine that it starts snowing during math class and six inches of snow quickly piles up outside. How would you convince your teacher to let you play outside in the snow?

 In what ways are snowflakes like people?

December 16

 Imagine that as you are sledding down a hill, you are suddenly in another world. Describe what you see there.

 Think about a time when you got hurt. Write about what happened.

December 17

✎ December 17 is Wright Brothers Day. Would you have liked to have been the first person to fly an airplane? Why or why not?

✎ What one thing would you like to be able to do that you cannot do now? Explain.

December 18

✎ Imagine that you found an old trunk in your grandmother's attic. Write about what happens next.

✎ What is your favorite holiday song? Why is it your favorite?

December 19

✎ Eve Bunting was born on December 19. She is the author of a book called *The Wednesday Surprise.* Imagine that you wake up to a surprise next Wednesday morning. Describe it.

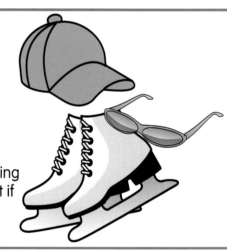

✎ Describe the silliest outfit that you can imagine wearing to school. How do you think your friends would react if you actually wore it?

December 20

✎ December is National Tie Month. Design a festive holiday tie. Describe what it looks like.

✎ Soon you will be leaving school for winter break. What will you miss most about school while you are away? Explain.

December 21

✏️ December is National Sign Up for Summer Camp Month. Explain why you think this special month is held in December.

✏️ Winter officially begins soon. Does this make you happy? Explain.

SUMMER CAMP

December 22

✏️ When exchanging presents with a friend, would you rather open your gift first or give your friend his or her gift first? Explain.

✏️ Imagine that you are in a toy store at closing. Suddenly you hear a toy plane whisper, "Is everyone gone?" A doll answers, "Yes!" Write about what happens next.

December 23

✏️ If you were a toy-making elf, what toy would you want to make? Explain.

✏️ Imagine that you are an evergreen tree on a Christmas tree lot. What would you say to convince a family to take you home to their house for the holidays?

December 24

BIG BOOK of REINDEER GAMES

✏️ In the Christmas song "Rudolph the Red-Nosed Reindeer," there is talk of reindeer games. What kinds of games do you think reindeer would play? Explain.

✏️ Sometimes it is hard waiting for special days or events. What can you do to make the waiting easier? Explain.

December 25

✏️ Describe your perfect Christmas morning.

✏️ Would you rather live in a location that gets a lot of snow or no snow at all? Explain.

December 26

✏️ Kwanzaa starts today. This is a festival in which some Black Americans celebrate the importance of family. Explain what makes your family so important to you.

✏️ Today is Boxing Day in Canada and in the United Kingdom. This holiday began as a way to give gifts to people who serve the public, such as a postal worker and a trash collector. What present would you give your mail carrier and why?

December 27

✏️ Louis Pasteur was born on December 27, 1822. He developed a way to make milk safe to drink. How would you feel if you had to stop drinking milk completely? Explain.

✏️ Write a story about you and your best friend, a snowpal.

December 28

✏️ Imagine that you find a jar of glittery sand on your doorstep with instructions to sprinkle it around your house. Write about what happens next.

✏️ What would you do if you got a gift that you did not like? Explain.

December 29

✏ A filmmaker wants to make a movie about your life. Write a list of possible titles for the film.

✏ Describe your favorite toy.

December 30

✏ December 30 is No Interruptions Day. Do you think there are good interruptions? Explain.

✏ Today is author Mercer Mayer's birthday. He wrote the popular books *There's a Nightmare in My Closet* and *There's an Alligator Under My Bed*. Select one of these titles and change *Nightmare* or *Alligator* to another word. Then explain what the plot of your new book would be.

December 31

✏ Today is the last day of the year. What did you like most about this past year? Explain.

✏ December 31 is Make Up Your Mind Day. Write about a time when it was difficult for you to make up your mind about something.

January 1

✎ Write three resolutions for the new year: one for home, one for school, and one for your community.

✎ If you could change one thing about last year, what would it be?

January 2

✎ Winter is a great time for warm soup. Describe your favorite soup.

✎ Would you rather be a bird that lives in cold, snowy weather or a bird that migrates south for the winter? Why?

January 3

✎ Describe your favorite winter meal.

✎ Imagine that the moon tucks you into bed at night. Write a bedtime song that the moon sings to you.

January 4

✎ Jacob Grimm was born on January 4, 1785. He and his brother wrote a collection of fairy tales. Think of a fairy tale you enjoy, and write a new ending for it.

✎ Describe the most beautiful place you have ever seen.

January 5

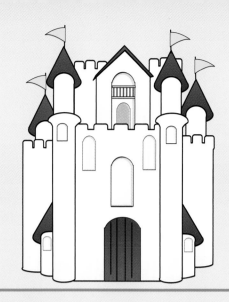

✎ The first Monday in January is Organize Your Home Day. What area of your bedroom needs to be organized the most? Describe what you can do to organize it and keep it that way.

✎ Imagine you are the leader of a secret kingdom under your bed. Describe your kingdom and the creatures in it.

January 6

✎ January is Oatmeal Month. Imagine that as you stir your oatmeal, it begins to turn strange colors. Write about what happens next.

✎ What is your favorite thing about you? Why do you find this trait special?

January 7

✎ You are now one week into the new year. Is the year starting off on the right foot? Explain.

✎ Imagine you live in a castle made entirely of ice. Describe a day in your life.

January 8

✎ How have computers and technology changed the way we communicate with each other? Explain.

✎ Write a letter to an alien persuading him to fly you to his planet for a month.

JANUARY

January 9

✏ Write directions for making hot chocolate.

✏ If you could bring to life any object in your desk at school, which object would you choose? Explain.

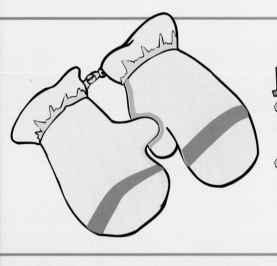

January 10

✏ Would you rather go skiing or sledding in the snow? Explain.

✏ Imagine that you lost your mittens. Create a poster describing them. Include your name as well as a reward for returning them.

January 11

✏ Icy winter weather can cause power failures. If you had no electricity, explain how you would keep warm on a freezing day.

✏ Describe how you think it would feel to sled down an entire mountain.

January 12

✏ The second Monday in January is National Clean Off Your Desk Day. What interesting things do you think you would find if you cleaned off your teacher's desk?

✏ If your desk could talk, what would it say to you? How would you respond?

January 13

 You are an inventor who just created a pair of boots with special powers. Describe what your boots can do.

 You just counted the money in your change jar and you have $32! What will you do with the money?

January 14

 Make a list of clothes you need outside on a snowy day. Then imagine you do not have the last three items on the list. How do you use what you have to stay warm?

 Pretend that mittens do not have a thumb. What activities will be difficult to do?

January 15

 Martin Luther King Jr. was born on this day. He is famous for his peaceful attempts to bring equality to all people. How can you be a more peaceful person?

 Write a poem about peace.

January 16

 January 16 is National Nothing Day. How long do you think it takes to become tired of doing nothing? What would you rather do instead of doing nothing?

 Pretend you find a penguin in Florida. How will you take care of it until it can be returned home?

JANUARY

January 17

✏ Benjamin Franklin was born on this day in 1706. During a thunderstorm, Franklin proved that lightning is electricity. Compare lightning to your bedroom light. In what ways are they alike? In what ways are they different?

✏ If you could do anything you wanted today, what would it be? Explain.

January 18

✏ January 18 is Pooh Day in honor of author A. A. Milne. Which Pooh character are you most like? Explain why.

✏ Would you rather be a cactus or an evergreen tree? Explain.

January 19

✏ The tin can was patented on this day in 1825. What is your favorite food that comes in a can? Describe how you like to eat this food.

✏ If you could change one thing about school, what would it be? How would this change affect others at your school?

Tasty! **Sweet Peas**

January 20

✏ January is Walk Your Pet Month. Why is it important to walk your pet? How do you benefit from the walks as well?

✏ Imagine that your dog runs away while you are walking him. You finally find him in the woods an hour later, but now you are lost. Write about what happens next.

January 21

✎ January 21 is Squirrel Appreciation Day. How can you celebrate this day?

✎ Today is National Hugging Day. Write about a time when you really needed a hug.

January 22

✎ January 22 is Answer Your Cat's Question Day. How would a city cat's questions be different from a farm cat's questions?

✎ Would you rather be a cat or a mouse? Explain.

January 23

✎ Today is National Handwriting Day in honor of John Hancock's birthday. Hancock was the first person to sign the Declaration of Independence, and he made his signature very large and easy to read. Give three examples of when it is important to write clearly.

✎ Do you prefer to type on a computer or write with a pen or pencil? Explain.

January 24

✎ What colors, items, and people do you associate with joy and happiness? Explain.

✎ Write a tale titled "How the Wind Came to Howl."

January 25

✎ January is National High-Tech Month. How does technology make your life easier?

✎ In your opinion, what is the best invention? Explain.

January 26

✎ If you could play any instrument, which one would you choose? Why?

✎ Compare a day in January to a day in June.

January 27

✎ Which do you enjoy watching more: summer sports or winter sports? Explain.

✎ Write a letter to Jack Frost. Tell him whether you would like him to stay longer this year or go away until next winter. Give at least three reasons for your request.

January 28

✎ The Super Bowl is held this time of year. Will you watch the game? If so, who will you cheer for and why? If not, what will you do instead of watching the game?

✎ National Compliment Day is held on the fourth Wednesday in January. List five people you will see today. Write a separate compliment for each person.

January 29

✏ Write a list of tools that people use in the snow. Imagine that each of these came to life. Write about what happens next.

✏ Imagine that you woke up this morning and found out that you were snowed in. What could you do to pass the time indoors?

January 30

✏ The last Friday in January is Fun at Work Day. How can you make today fun for your teacher?

✏ Pretend that you are a pair of ice skates. Write about your day on the ice.

January 31

✏ January is Family Fit Lifestyle Month. Did your family work together to stay healthy this month? If so, give some examples of your actions. If not, write what you can do to be a fit family during the month of February.

✏ When sharing a project with the class, do you prefer to go first or last?

February 1

✏️ Write about a time you helped a family member cook something. Tell about your job, what you made, and how the item turned out.

✏️ Pretend that it is up to you to choose a new name for February. What name will you give it? Why?

February 2

✏️ Oh no! All of the groundhogs are missing! Tell where they could be and what they are doing.

✏️ Which would you prefer to do: be invisible or fly like a bird? Why?

February 3

✏️ The first woman doctor, Elizabeth Blackwell, was born on this date in 1821. Doctors should be caring, whether they are male or female. What other qualities should a doctor have?

✏️ The coldest temperature in North America—81° below zero (Fahrenheit)—was recorded in Canada's Yukon Territory on this date in 1947. How do you think the animals there kept themselves warm on that date?

February 4

✏️ Charles Lindbergh, the first person to fly solo across the Atlantic Ocean without stopping, was born on this date in 1902. Pretend that you are the reporter who interviewed him after his journey. Write three questions that you asked Lindbergh.

✏️ Which would you prefer to do: help with the laundry or help with the yard work?

February 5

✎ John Jeffries, one of the first Americans to keep a record of weather conditions, was born on this day in 1744. Write three questions Jeffries might ask a modern weatherperson.

✎ Which type of weather do you think mail carriers prefer: rain or snow? Explain.

February 6

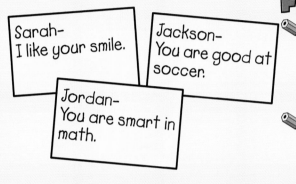

✎ Pay-a-Compliment Day is February 6. Write a compliment for three different classmates. When you have a chance, read each person's compliment to him or her!

✎ Suppose that your sled understands your thoughts and knows how fast and where you want it to go. Describe how it will take you down a hill the next time it snows.

February 7

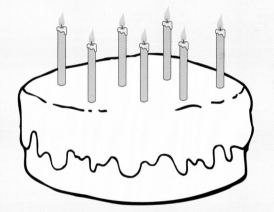

✎ Laura Ingalls Wilder was born on this day in 1867. Pretend that you are Laura. Write a diary entry that tells what you did on your birthday.

✎ Would you rather sleep in a tent in the country or in a motel room in the city? Explain.

February 8

✎ February is National Children's Dental Health Month. Write the steps a person should follow to brush his or her teeth.

✎ If you could be any animal for a day, which animal would you choose to be? Explain.

February 9

✎ February is Library Lovers' Month. What do you like best about your town's public library? What do you like least? Explain.

✎ Fun hobbies include playing basketball, collecting sports cards, learning ballet, and practicing magic tricks. If you were going to start a new hobby, what would it be? Why?

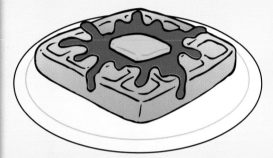

February 10

✎ Pretend that you own a restaurant. Create three different menus of hot breakfast foods that any child your age would love to eat.

✎ Where would you prefer your family to live: in a desert or in a rain forest? Explain.

February 11

✎ The famous inventor Thomas Edison was born on this day in 1847. Describe an invention that could be made by combining two of the following items: cup, mirror, clock, chair, refrigerator, magnet, or glasses. Include a drawing of the invention.

✎ Describe how you think a bird feels after a deep snow has fallen. How would a rabbit feel?

February 12

✎ Abraham Lincoln's birthday—February 12—is also Lost Penny Day. You might have heard the saying "Find a penny; pick it up. All day long you'll have good luck!" Pretend you have just found a penny. Describe the good luck that the penny brings your way.

✎ Red can be a popular color in February. There are red hearts, candies, and roses. List five more things that are red. Tell how each object is different from the others.

February 13

✏️ Pretend that an alien is coming to your house for dinner tonight. Make a list of dos and don'ts about table manners so the alien will know how to behave.

✏️ Which would you rather do to help with a meal: set the table or clear it? Explain.

February 14

✏️ Happy Valentine's Day! Use the letters in the word *valentine* to form six different words. Use the words to help you write a valentine message to Cupid.

✏️ Ferris wheels go round and round. Make a list of other things that go around.

February 15

✏️ February is Black History Month. Pretend that you are on the committee that will decide which famous Black Americans will have their likenesses appear on postage stamps. Which person will you select? Why?

✏️ Chocolate is a favorite treat of many people. Describe your favorite way to eat chocolate.

February 16

✏️ Presidents' Day is celebrated each year on the third Monday in February. If you could meet any president, whom would you want to meet? Why?

✏️ Write three silly reasons that explain why doughnuts have holes.

FEBRUARY

February 17

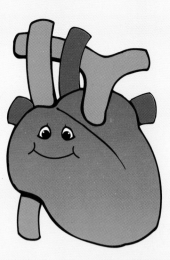

✏️ February is American Heart Month. What kinds of things can you do to try to keep your heart healthy?

✏️ Pretend that your best friend wants to become a doctor. What advice could you give to him or her?

February 18

✏️ Wow! Every time you put your hand in your coat pocket, you pull out a different item. What would you most like to pull out of this magic pocket? Explain.

✏️ How do computers make your life different?

February 19

✏️ Imagine that you took a nap and slept for 100 years. Describe what the world is like when you awake that many years in the future.

✏️ Sometimes a baseball coach might say to a player, "Keep your eye on the ball." What advice could you give yourself that might help you have a successful day at school?

A+

February 20

✏️ What could you say to a classmate who is having trouble in math to help him or her feel better?

✏️ Pretend that at sundown each night you are able to talk to animals. What might your favorite animal say to you? What would you say to it?

Male lions are the only cats with manes.

February 21

✎ What are your daily tasks? List them. Include the time you need to complete each one. Then explain what you could do if you have any extra time on your hands.

✎ What is the best thing that has ever happened to you at school? Write about it. Include what happened before and after the event.

February 22

✎ George Washington, our country's first president, was born on this date in 1732. Streets and schools are named after him. His likeness appears on the dollar bill. Would you like to be honored in such ways? Why or why not?

✎ Describe five different foods that can be made with cherries.

February 23

✎ Think of a book you have read that you wished had a different ending. Write the title of the book. Then write a new ending for the story.

✎ A paper clip can be used to hold papers together. What other uses can it have? List as many different uses for a paper clip as you can.

February 24

✎ What would you do if you saw someone take a pack of gum from a store without paying for it?

✎ Cupcake and grapefruit are two compound words that name foods. List three more foods whose names are compound words. Then use all five foods to create a recipe for a wacky new food.

F
E
B
R
U
A
R
Y

FEBRUARY

February 25

✏️ Pretend that you have a friend who lives in a different part of the world. What could your friend teach you about his or her country that you might not learn from a book?

✏️ How important is it that a good friend be a good listener? Explain.

February 26

✏️ Describe how you could help an elderly person during the cold weather months.

✏️ Which would you rather have: free movie passes, a new book, or a puppy? Explain.

February 27

✏️ Suppose that a huge blizzard will bring so much snow to your town that people will not be able to leave their homes for days. Explain how you and your family would get ready for such a storm.

✏️ If you could set your own bedtime, what time would you go to bed? Describe how you would spend your time from dinner until bedtime.

February 28

✏️ Pretend that your parent has said that you can have the playroom of your dreams. Describe what color it will be and the kind of furniture it will have.

✏️ Which task do you think would be harder to do: caring for a human baby or caring for a puppy? Why?

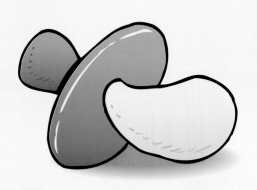

February 29

✏️ Every four years, February has 29 days instead of 28. The 29th day is called Leap Year Day. How could someone born on Leap Year Day celebrate his or her birthday each year?

✏️ Some animals, such as frogs, can leap. List more animals that can leap.

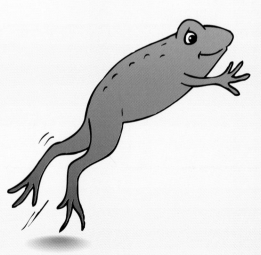

March 1

✎ Today is National Pig Day. Change the underlined word in the first line of the popular children's rhyme that begins "This Little Piggy Went to <u>Market</u>." Change the words to the rest of the rhyme to fit your new line.

✎ Which of the seven dwarfs are you most like: Sleepy, Grumpy, Happy, Doc, Dopey, Sneezy, or Bashful? Explain.

March 2

✎ Today is Dr. Seuss's birthday. He is the author of *And to Think That I Saw It on Mulberry Street*. Pretend that you are walking down Mulberry Street. Write about what you see that is so unusual.

✎ The first full week in March is Newspaper in Education Week. Would you rather write articles for, take pictures for, or deliver the newspaper? Explain.

March 3

✎ Alexander Graham Bell, inventor of the telephone, was born on March 3, 1847. If you could call anyone in the world, whom would you call? Explain.

✎ For each letter in the word *happy*, describe something that makes you happy.

March 4

✎ The first full week in March is National School Breakfast Week. Do you prefer a hot or cold breakfast? Explain.

✎ Describe three or more ways that marching in a parade and running in a race are alike.

March 5

✎ March is National Umbrella Month. Pretend that you open your umbrella and it starts to lift you up into the air. Write about what happens next.

✎ What could you say to someone to convince him or her that March is the best month of the year? Give three or more reasons.

March 6

✎ March is Optimism Month. An optimistic person looks for the positive side of each situation. Imagine that you got a piece of gum stuck in your hair. Write about how this turned into a positive experience.

✎ Pretend that you own a pair of shoes that makes you become invisible. Write about a day you spent wearing your new shoes.

March 7

✎ Save Your Vision Week is the first week in March. What three things can you do to keep your eyes safe?

✎ Imagine that you found a ladder that leads up to a cloud. You begin to climb the ladder. What happens next?

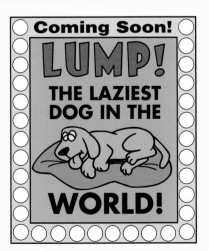

March 8

✎ Would you rather go to the movie theater or watch a movie at home? Explain.

✎ Write about what you think your teacher does at school before you arrive and after you leave for the day.

March 9

Welcome to
SCRATCH ANKLE
pop. 2045

✎ Unique Names Day is held during the first week in March. Scratch Ankle, Cookietown, Surprise, Pitchfork, Toast, and Frog Jump are all actual names of U.S. towns. Choose one name from the list and make up a story about how the town got its name.

✎ Do you think it is more difficult to be a teacher or a student? Explain.

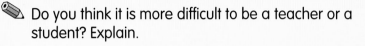

March 10

✎ U.S. paper money was first issued on March 10, 1862. Imagine that a law was passed to stop using paper money and use only coins. How might life change?

✎ If a raindrop could talk, what do you think it would say? Write a conversation between a raindrop and another object or person.

March 11

✎ Do you think it is more important to keep a secret or to keep a friend? Explain.

✎ During March, many people focus on the sport of basketball. If you could change the focus of March to another sport or topic, what would you choose? Explain.

March 12

✎ Pretend that you are so small you can be carried around in someone's hand. Write a story about spending a day as this tiny person.

✎ Imagine that you are a farmer. Suddenly your cow is giving chocolate milk and your chickens are laying hard-boiled eggs. Write a silly story about this mixed-up day on the farm.

March 13

✎ Imagine that you have been chosen to be the substitute teacher for your class. How will this school day be different than others?

✎ Are you more like thunder or lightning? Explain.

March 14

✎ Imagine that you just put on your new hat and you suddenly became something else. Write about what happens next.

✎ Would you rather visit a garden during spring or a forest in the fall? Explain.

March 15

✎ The third Monday in March is Act Happy Day. Without speaking, how can you let others know that you are happy? Write five or more ways.

✎ Imagine that in the middle of your math lesson a leprechaun strolls into your room. Write about what happens next.

March 16

✎ March is National Nutrition Month. Write a menu for a healthy breakfast, lunch, and dinner.

✎ Pretend that you are the richest person in the world. Describe one day in your life.

March 17

✏️ Today is St. Patrick's Day. Imagine that you just found a four-leaf clover. Write about how your luck has suddenly started to change.

✏️ Make a list of ten or more green things. If you could change the color of one of those things, which would you choose? Explain.

March 18

✏️ Tell about a time when you were embarrassed.

✏️ If you had to leave home and could take only one object, what would you take? Explain.

March 19

✏️ What should someone suffering from spring fever do for a cure?

✏️ National Poison Prevention Week is held the third full week of March. Imagine that you have been asked to create a poster to remind other students about the dangers of poisoning. What would you write on your poster?

March 20

✏️ Describe what you think about when you think of spring.

✏️ National Agriculture Day is celebrated on the first day of spring. Would you rather be a farmer or a teacher? Explain.

March 21

Would you rather visit Hawaii or Alaska? Explain.

Pretend that you could build a house using any one building material, such as candy, wood, or baseball cards. What would you use to build your house? Explain.

March 22

Today is International Goof-Off Day. Why do you think someone made this special day?

Spring has officially sprung! Imagine that you have suddenly sprung springs on your feet. Describe how you spend the day bouncing around.

March 23

The word *OK* first appeared in print on March 23, 1839. The words *book*, *Oklahoma*, and *joke* all have the letter combination *ok* in them. List as many words as you can that have that letter combination. Then write a poem using some of the words.

Would you rather be a turtle or a rabbit? Explain.

March 24

March is International Listening Awareness Month. Sit quietly with your eyes closed for a minute or two. Write a paragraph describing all the sounds you hear around you.

Would you rather drive a fire truck or an ambulance? Explain.

March 25

✏ March is Music in Our Schools Month. Write three or more things that you can do today to be sure that someone hears music.

✏ Choose two musical instruments. Tell how they are alike and how they are different.

March 26

✏ Imagine that each time you open your umbrella something unusual happens. Write about one of those times.

✏ Would you rather watch your favorite cartoon or read a comic book? Explain.

March 27

✏ Youth Art Month is observed in March. How would you feel if your school suddenly banned any kind of art? Explain.

✏ Imagine that you are a bird just returning home after flying south for the winter. What tasks are on your to-do list?

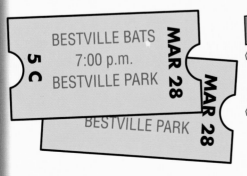

BESTVILLE BATS
7:00 p.m.
BESTVILLE PARK

5 C

MAR 28

MAR 28

BESTVILLE PARK

MAR 28

March 28

✏ Pretend that you are going to start a garden. Write directions telling how you would do this.

✏ Baseball is sometimes called the national pastime. Explain why you think this is so.

March 29

 National Cleaning Week is the last week in March. What is your favorite cleaning chore? What is your least favorite? Explain.

 Imagine that you find a set of muddy footprints leading across your kitchen floor. Write about where the prints lead and who created them.

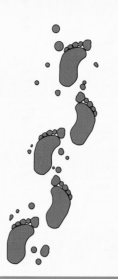

March 30

 Today is Doctors' Day. If you were a doctor, would you rather work with children or adults? Explain.

 The pencil with an eraser was patented on March 30, 1858. What other things can be done to improve the pencil?

March 31

 Are you more like a lion or a lamb? Explain.

 Which grocery store aisle is your favorite? Explain.

MARCH

April 1

✏️ Think about an April Fools' Day prank that has been played on you or a friend. Write a description of it and explain whether it was funny or not.

✏️ April is School Library Media Month. Write a description of what a school library might look like in the future.

April 2

✏️ Nickelodeon, the cable TV channel for kids, debuted on April 2, 1979. Imagine that you could create your own TV show. Describe what it would be like.

✏️ Make up silly new lyrics to a familiar tune such as "London Bridge" or "Old MacDonald Had a Farm."

April 3

✏️ List four colors you think of when you think of spring. Write a descriptive sentence using each color.

✏️ *Splash* and *plop* are examples of *onomatopoeia*, words that are spelled like the sounds they make. Write five more spring sound words. Then use your words in a paragraph.

April 4

✏️ April is National Humor Month. Write your favorite joke. Tell about the first time you heard this joke.

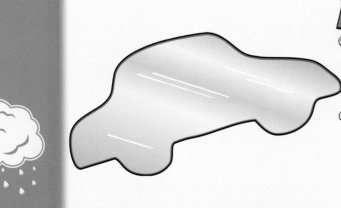

✏️ Imagine that you could see pictures in puddles just as some people see pictures in clouds. Draw a picture of a strangely shaped puddle and write about what you see in it.

April 5

 Describe your favorite thing to do outside when the weather turns warm.

 Imagine that you took the place of the Easter Bunny this year. Write about an adventure you had while making a delivery.

April 6

 Pretend you could fill your own Easter basket. What items would you put in it? Explain why you chose each one.

Many things in nature change during spring. Describe three of these changes.

April 7

 Should you get paid for helping with spring cleaning at your house? Explain why you should or shouldn't.

If you had to be outside in a heavy downpour, would you rather have a raincoat or an umbrella?

April 8

 April is National Lawn and Garden Month. Design a wanted poster for a garden pest such as a weed.

 Write about an unexpected day of snow after a week of warm spring weather.

April 9

✏️ Design an outrageous springtime hat and write the steps to make it.

✏️ Write a story about finding something amazing while you are digging in your garden.

April 10

✏️ Today is National Siblings Day. What are the qualities of a good brother or sister?

✏️ The safety pin was patented on this day in 1849. Pretend you are a safety pin. Write about one of your adventures.

April 11

✏️ April is National Poetry Month. What do you think are the easiest and the hardest things about writing a poem? Explain.

✏️ Baseball season starts in the spring. Would you rather be a baseball, a bat, or a glove?

April 12

✏️ Today is author Beverly Cleary's birthday. Many of her books have children as main characters. What event from your life would make a good chapter for a Beverly Cleary book?

✏️ National Garden Week is the second full week in April. Draw and describe your dream garden.

A P R I L

April 13

✏ April is National Soft Pretzel Month. Write a recipe for an unusual soft pretzel topping.

✏ Write about a special spring memory. Include a detail for each of your five senses.

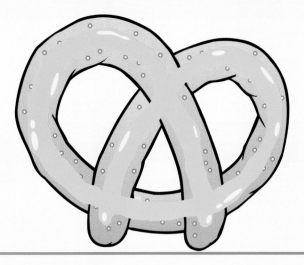

April 14

✏ Today is Anne Sullivan's birthday. She taught Helen Keller to use language even though Helen couldn't see, hear, or speak. Explain how you would teach someone to do something difficult.

✏ Write about what might happen if it didn't rain in spring.

April 15

✏ The first McDonald's restaurant opened on this day in 1955. Write an original jingle or sales slogan for your favorite fast-food product.

✏ Imagine that you are a bird. Write the steps for building your nest.

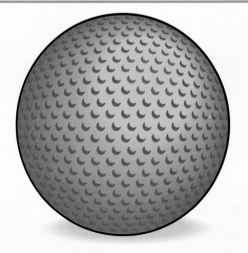

April 16

✏ Today is National Wear Your Pajamas to Work Day! Write about what would happen if your principal wore his or her pajamas to school.

✏ What is your favorite playground game? Explain how it is played.

A
P
R
I
L

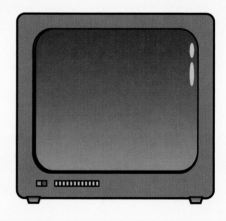

April 17

✏️ Earth Day is celebrated in April. Write an invitation to a party for the earth.

✏️ Describe your favorite springtime scent and explain why it's your favorite.

April 18

✏️ Design your own coin. Explain why you chose each symbol on it.

✏️ Imagine that you are a butterfly that has just emerged from its cocoon. Write about what happens next.

April 19

✏️ Would it be hard for you to turn your television off for a whole week? Explain.

✏️ What celebrity would you most like to resemble and why?

April 20

✏️ April is National Woodworking Month. If you could make objects from wood, would you rather make useful objects or beautiful ones? Why?

✏️ List three important library rules and why they are important.

A P R I L

April 21

✏️ Today is Kindergarten Day. Describe your favorite kindergarten memory.

✏️ Would you rather be a duck on a pond or a butterfly in the air? Explain.

April 22

✏️ Name one thing you would like to save money to buy. Then write a plan for saving the money.

✏️ The fourth Thursday in April is Take Our Daughters and Sons to Work Day. Write about what you think it would be like to spend a day at work with one of your parents.

April 23

✏️ The first movie theater opened on April 23, 1896. Describe an idea you have for a new movie and the actors you would want to star in it.

✏️ On this day in 1635, the first American public school opened. Imagine what a day in that school might have been like and write a schedule for that day.

April 24

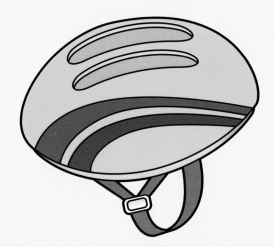

✏️ Design your own constellation by drawing stars and connecting them like a dot-to-dot puzzle. Then describe your constellation and give it a name.

✏️ April is National Youth Sports Safety Month. List five or more ways that you can stay safe while playing your favorite sport.

A P R I L

April 25

 April 25 is the anniversary of Earth Day. Describe to an alien why our planet needs to be protected.

 On this day in 1901, New York became the first state to require licenses on cars. Design a personalized license plate for yourself or a friend. Describe what it looks like.

April 26

 Today is John Audubon's birthday. He was a famous naturalist who studied living things. If you were a naturalist, would you rather study plants or animals? Explain.

 If you were a plant, would you rather be a plant that produces vegetables or one that produces only flowers? Explain.

April 27

 National Playground Safety Week is in April. List the three most important rules for staying safe on a playground. Explain why each rule is important.

 Write a make-believe story to explain why there is thunder and lightning during a storm.

April 28

 April is Prevention of Animal Cruelty Month. Pretend you are a pet. Write a letter to your owner explaining how to care for you.

 April is National Kite Month. Pretend you are a kite and write a weather report for perfect kite-flying weather.

April 29

✏️ On this day in 1913, the zipper was patented. Write about what might happen if all the zippers in the world suddenly got stuck.

✏️ Write a review that will convince your best friend to watch your favorite movie.

April 30

✏️ National Arbor Day is celebrated on the last Friday in April. Imagine that you have adopted a tree. What kind of tree is it, and how will you care for it?

✏️ April 30 is National Honesty Day. Write about a time when it was hard to be honest. What happened? How would the situation have changed if you hadn't been honest?

A P R I L

May 1

 Today is School Principals' Day. Describe what you would do if you were principal of your school for a day.

✎ May 1 is Mother Goose Day. Write a short conversation between two characters from two different nursery rhymes.

May 2

✎ List three things you appreciate about your brother or sister, or write a description of an ideal brother or sister.

✎ May is Clean Air Month. Why do you think it is important to have clean air?

May 3

 Why do you think that dessert is usually served at the end of a meal?

✎ Describe something you miss about winter.

May 4

✎ The first full week of May is Be Kind to Animals Week. Pretend that you are an animal. List three or more ways that someone could be kind to you.

✎ Make a list of three people that you admire. Choose one and explain why you would like to be more like that person.

Mom is special!

1.

2.

3.

4.

5.

May 5

 The first full week of May is National Family Week. Pretend that you are another member of your family. Describe your new role.

 The second Sunday in May is Mother's Day. List five or more special things about your mom or another special woman in your life.

May 6

 Today is No Homework Day! Imagine that your teacher decided to celebrate this day by not assigning any homework. What would you do with the extra time?

 May 6 is author Leo Lionni's birthday. In many of his books, the main character learns to believe in himself. Write about one time when you believed in yourself.

No Homework Tonight

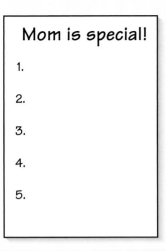

HELP WANTED

May 7

 National Pet Week is the first full week in May. Write a "Help Wanted" ad for the perfect pet owner.

 Pretend that your teacher has told you that you can skip two grade levels and join a new class on Monday. Explain how you feel.

May 8

 Pretend you are a bird who flew north for the summer. Write a postcard to a friend who stayed in the south.

 The Saturday before Mother's Day is National Baby-sitters Day. Write a list of babysitter dos and don'ts.

May 9

✎ Would you rather be a caterpillar or a butterfly? Explain.

✎ Write about a way you could make a friend or family member's day.

May 10

✎ If you were a superhero, what special power would you like to have? Explain.

✎ Describe your favorite daydream.

May 11

✎ Today is Eat What You Want Day. Write a menu for the perfect breakfast, lunch, and dinner.

✎ Imagine that you just answered the phone and you cannot believe the voice you hear. Who has called? Write about your conversation.

May 12

✎ May is National Bike Month. Write directions for how to ride a bike.

✎ Compare a toy doll to a toy car. In what ways are they alike? In what ways are they different?

M
A
Y

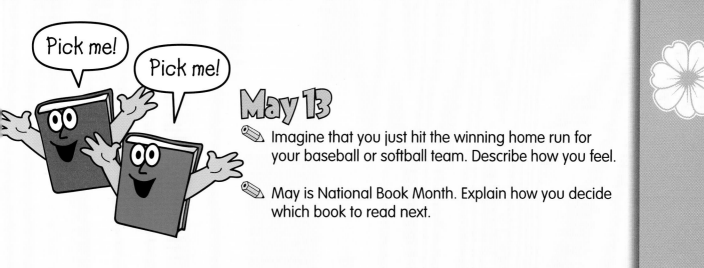

 Pick me!

Pick me!

May 13

 Imagine that you just hit the winning home run for your baseball or softball team. Describe how you feel.

Imagine that you just hit the winning home run for your baseball or softball team. Describe how you feel.

May is National Book Month. Explain how you decide which book to read next.

May 14

 Imagine that you were weeding in the garden when you spotted a hidden door in the ground. Write about what happens when you open the door.

Would you rather take a ride on a train or a boat? Explain.

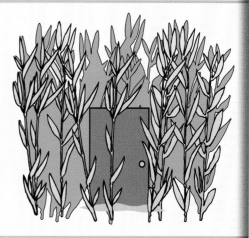

May 15

How would you feel if Christmas was in May instead of December?

Create a new recipe that has chocolate chips in it. Describe what it tastes like.

May 16

May is National Egg Month. Write a silly story explaining why eggs are sold by the dozen.

Describe the best dream you've ever had.

Grade A Eggs

May 17

✎ Describe the best gift you ever received. Tell who gave it and when you received it.

✎ What is your favorite amusement park ride? Explain.

GYMNASTICS

May 18

✎ Today is Visit Your Relatives Day. Which relative would you most like to visit? Explain.

✎ May 18 is International Museum Day. What one item of yours would you like to display in a museum? Explain.

May 19

✎ Do you prefer your bedroom to be messy or neat? Explain.

✎ Describe your favorite type of candy without giving away its name.

May 20

✎ Write about your favorite way to stay cool in warm weather.

✎ What type of hidden treasure would you most like to find? Where would you find it?

M
A
Y

May 21

✏️ May is National Hamburger Month. Describe the perfect way to top a hamburger.

✏️ Pretend that you are a new animal in the zoo. How could the other zoo animals make you feel welcome?

May 22

✏️ May is Older Americans Month. Write five questions that you would like to ask someone about the olden days.

✏️ What is your favorite party game? Explain how to play it.

May 23

✏️ Today is World Turtle Day. Pretend that you are the tortoise in "The Tortoise and the Hare." Describe the race from your point of view.

✏️ List five or more things you would like to learn about in school next year.

May 24

✏️ Pretend that you are a photographer. What would you most like to take pictures of?

✏️ What are your favorite and least favorite things about writing in your journal? Explain.

May 25

✎ May is National Physical Fitness and Sports Month. List three or more ways you can keep your body in good shape.

✎ Imagine that you have $20 to spend. Would you rather buy one item that costs $20 or 20 items that each cost one dollar? Explain.

May 26

✎ Write about something that happened this school year that you will never forget.

✎ If you could meet any athlete, whom would you choose to meet? Explain.

May 27

✎ May is Young Achievers Month. List three or more goals that you have for the future.

✎ What is your favorite type of music? Compare it to your least favorite type of music.

May 28

✎ Imagine that you are a quintuplet, one of five children born at the same time. How do you feel about having four brothers or sisters the same age?

✎ What is your favorite vegetable? What is your least favorite? Explain.

May 29

✎ Many students take important school tests in May. List five or more ways to prepare for a test.

✎ Would you rather learn to play golf or tennis? Explain.

May 30

✎ If you could be famous for doing one thing, what would it be? Explain.

✎ If you could visit any planet in the solar system, which planet would you visit? Explain.

May 31

✎ May is almost over! What are you looking forward to in June?

✎ If you could paint your school classroom any color, what color would you choose? Explain.

LATEX
PAINT

June 1

✎ Imagine that you are going to meet the president of the United States. Write three or more questions that you would ask.

✎ Would you rather sit in a rocking chair or on a couch? Explain.

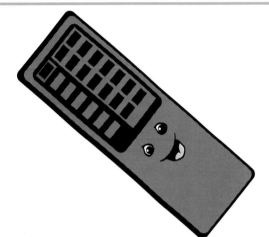

June 2

✎ Imagine that your best friend could spend the summer at your house. Describe how you would spend your time together.

✎ If you could make the remote control for your television control anything at all, what would you choose? Explain.

June 3

✎ If you could be any musical instrument, what would you be? Explain.

✎ Write about what happens to the single sock that never makes it out of the clothes dryer with its partner. Where does it go? What is it doing?

June 4

✎ Imagine that you are a fly that can sit on any wall and hear other people talking without them knowing that you are listening. On which wall would you like to sit? Explain.

✎ June is National Rose Month. If you could give a single rose to any one person, who would you choose? Explain.

June 5

✎ Which number has special meaning to you? Explain.

✎ June is Student Safety Month. What would you tell a kindergarten class about how to be safe at school? Give at least three safety tips.

June 6

✎ Describe one day at the perfect summer camp.

✎ It is time to celebrate June Dairy Month. Write a note to a cow thanking her for the milk she gives.

June 7

✎ Some animals sleep during the day and are awake at night. How would school be different if it was held during the night?

✎ Do you prefer Saturdays or Sundays? Explain.

June 8

✎ Imagine that you were asked to design a new pair of shoes. Describe what the shoes look like.

✎ Would you rather be an octopus or a shark? Explain.

June 9

✏️ June 9 is Donald Duck's birthday. Who do you think Donald would like to invite to his birthday party? Explain.

✏️ If you could change the color of your hair, would you? Explain why or why not.

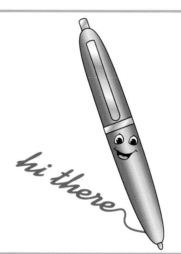

June 10

✏️ Maurice Sendak, author of *Where the Wild Things Are*, was born on June 10. Write a silly story about a time when you found some wild things.

✏️ The ballpoint pen was patented on June 10, 1943. Imagine that your pen suddenly comes to life while you are writing. Write about what happens next.

June 11

✏️ Imagine that you are a seed. Would you rather be planted in a garden, in a park, or in a flower pot? Explain.

✏️ June is National Candy Month. Imagine that candy was suddenly banned. Explain how you would feel.

June 12

✏️ Imagine that you could teach someone about any topic in the world. What would you like to teach? Explain.

✏️ Would you like to be famous? Explain.

June 13

✎ Describe how you would design the perfect bicycle.

✎ Would you rather watch the sunrise in the morning or the sunset in the evening? Explain.

June 14

✎ June 14 is Flag Day. Imagine that you have been asked to redesign the U.S. flag. Describe how you would like it to look.

✎ Imagine that you have figured out a way to make the world's weather the same every day. Describe how you would like the weather to be. Explain why you chose this type of weather.

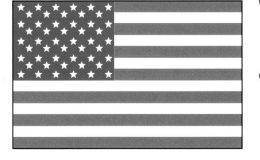

June 15

✎ Would you rather be Batman or Superman? Explain.

✎ Pretend that you are a puppy at a pet store. Describe what you would do to convince someone to take you home.

June 16

✎ Would you rather own a bird or a lizard as a pet? Explain.

✎ Describe how school would be different if your building did not have electricity.

June 17

✏️ Father's Day is the third Sunday in June. Explain what it means to be a father.

✏️ Imagine that you could snap your fingers and be any age. How old would you like to be? Explain.

HAPPY FATHER'S DAY, DAD!

Love, Steve

June 18

✏️ Author Chris Van Allsburg was born on June 18. He wrote the book *Two Bad Ants*. What might a story titled "Two Good Ants" be about?

✏️ Some professional sports players make millions of dollars each year. Do you think this is too much money for playing sports? Explain.

June 19

✏️ Would you rather be the oldest or youngest child in the family? Explain.

✏️ Imagine that the food in your refrigerator comes to life when you shut the door. Write a story about what happens inside.

June 20

✏️ Pretend that you are a gift that was just given to someone. Explain how you feel.

✏️ Explain what you think is meant by the saying "You have eyes in the back of your head."

June 21

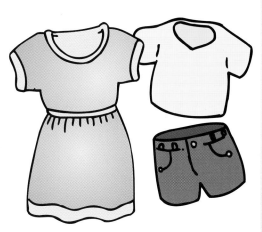

✎ Would you rather wear dress clothes or play clothes? Explain.

✎ Imagine that you could plant a tree that could grow any object on it. What would you like your tree to grow? Explain.

June 22

✎ Would you rather visit the beach in the summer or the mountains in the fall? Explain.

✎ If you could change the color of the sky, which color would you choose? Explain.

June 23

✎ If goldfish could dream, what do you think they would dream about? Explain.

✎ Write a silly story about why piggy banks are pigs.

June 24

✎ Would you rather eat an ice pop or an ice-cream cone? Explain.

✎ What is your favorite restaurant? Explain.

JUNE

June 25

✏️ June is Turkey Lovers' Month. Are you a turkey lover? Explain.

✏️ If you could star in any kind of movie, would you choose action, comedy, or drama? Explain.

June 26

✏️ Imagine that you are in charge of your family's dinner menu for an entire week. What could you eat on each of the seven days?

✏️ Write a silly story about why zebras have stripes.

June 27

✏️ Would you rather paint a picture or sculpt something out of clay? Explain.

✏️ Write about a time when you had plans to go somewhere and you didn't get to go. How did you feel?

June 28

✏️ Would you rather walk outside barefoot or wear shoes? Explain.

✏️ Imagine that a rabbit hopped up to you and started talking. Write about your conversation.

June 29

 Imagine that your class is doing a play. Would you rather be the star actor, the writer, or the person who builds the sets? Explain.

 Would you rather be happy or rich? Explain.

June 30

 Write a poem titled "The Elephant and the Mouse."

 Are you more like a beach ball or a pool raft? Explain.

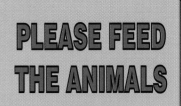
PLEASE FEED THE ANIMALS

July 1

 On July 1, 1874, the first U.S. zoo opened. Pretend that you are an animal in a zoo. Write about why zoo signs should read "Please Feed the Animals."

I Forgot Day is celebrated on the 183rd day each year. Write a paragraph that gives ideas and tips on how to not forget what you need to do.

July 2

 July is Cell Phone Courtesy Month. Do you think it is okay to use a cell phone in a store or a restaurant where others can hear what you are saying? Explain.

Imagine that you are a piece of seaweed floating on the ocean. Describe what you see as you float along.

July 3

The hot sun can be harmful to your body. How would you persuade your friends to come inside to play on a sunny day?

Pretend you are sending a message in a bottle to be put in the ocean. Write the note that you would send.

July 4

July 4 is Independence Day, our country's birthday. What gift would you like to give America for its birthday this year? Explain.

If you had a key to get into any door in the world, what would that door be and where would it lead? Explain.

July 5

✎ July is National Hot Dog Month. Would you rather eat a hot dog or a hamburger? Explain.

✎ Write a short newspaper article that you would like to have written about yourself in 20 years.

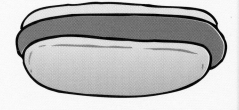

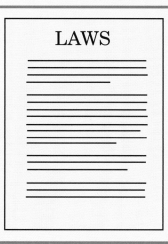

LAWS

July 6

✎ Imagine that you found a strange object in your pocket. Write about what happens next.

✎ Finish this sentence: "There should be a law against…" Explain.

July 7

✎ What advice would you give someone on how to make a new friend this summer?

✎ Pretend that you have a dog. Describe the perfect doghouse for him.

LAUGHTER

July 8

✎ Choose three words to describe yourself. Explain why you chose each word.

✎ What do you think the saying "Laughter is the best medicine" means? Do you agree?

July 9

✏️ July is National Recreation and Parks Month. Write a letter to park visitors encouraging them to keep the parks clean.

✏️ Imagine that you are staying at a hotel on a beach, and the hotel has a pool. Would you rather swim in the pool or in the ocean? Explain.

July 10

✏️ Imagine that you could put any message that you wanted on a billboard in your town. What message would you write? Explain.

✏️ Would you rather be a window or a door? Explain.

July 11

✏️ Pretend that you are on your dream vacation. Write a postcard to your best friend telling all about your trip.

✏️ Do you prefer lunch or dinner? Explain.

July 12

✏️ Would you like to be able to speak a language other than the one(s) you speak? Explain.

✏️ Write a silly story explaining how the giraffe got such a long neck.

July 13

✏️ Compare yourself to your best friend. Write about how you are alike and how you are different.

✏️ Would you rather ride in a small car or a large car? Explain.

July 14

✏️ Imagine that your pet (or a pet you know) could suddenly talk. Write three or more questions that you would ask it.

✏️ Describe your typical Sunday.

July 15

✏️ Are you more like a telephone or a computer? Explain.

✏️ Pretend that one night you and your friends get to stay up all night long. Write about how you would spend the time.

July 16

✏️ Do you think a parent should pay his or her child for doing chores? Explain.

✏️ Describe your favorite summertime memory.

July 17

✏ Disneyland opened on July 17, 1955. It was America's first theme park. Imagine that you were asked to design a theme park. What theme would you choose for your park? Explain.

✏ What is your favorite way to get exercise? Explain.

Hello

July 18

✏ The third Sunday in July is National Ice Cream Day. Make up a story telling how ice cream was first created.

✏ Imagine that you hold a large seashell to your ear and you hear a conversation. Who is talking? Write about what they are saying.

July 19

✏ Imagine that you are a grasshopper living in someone's backyard. Describe your typical day.

✏ Are you more like a sneaker or a flip-flop? Explain.

July 20

✏ Are you more like a lion, a deer, or a squirrel? Explain.

✏ Imagine that your neighbor asked you to baby-sit her pet hamster. Write about the funniest thing that happened while she was away.

July 21

✏️ Write about a lesson that you learned by watching a movie or reading a book.

✏️ Would you rather sleep late in the morning or stay up late at night? Explain.

July 22

✏️ Compare your classroom on the first day of school to the last day of school. Write about how it is the same and how it is different.

✏️ Pretend that there is a monster living under your bed. Write a letter convincing it to move.

July 23

✏️ Write about a dream that you have had. Do you think this dream would make a good movie? Why or why not?

✏️ Write about a time when you felt as if you didn't belong.

July 24

✏️ Which of your toys is hardest for you to share? Explain.

✏️ Would you rather be very strong or be able to run very fast? Explain.

July 25

🖉 Parents' Day is the fourth Sunday in July. Imagine that you are the parent and your parent is the child. Explain how things would be different in your house.

🖉 Would you rather smell fresh flowers or a home-cooked meal? Explain.

July 26

🖉 National Salad Week is held the last week in July. Would you rather eat a bowl of salad or a bowl of peas and carrots? Explain.

🖉 What one thing would you like to do better? Explain.

July 27

🖉 Imagine that you are old enough to have a summer job. What job would you like to have? Explain.

🖉 Do you like thunderstorms? Explain.

July 28

🖉 Would you rather be a firefly or a frog? Explain.

🖉 Write a letter to the principal of your school persuading him or her to make summer vacation longer or shorter. Give three or more reasons in your letter.

July 29

 Pretend that you are a fish. Write a letter convincing your town to post a "No Fishing" sign at your lake.

 How might our country be different if there were no laws? Explain.

July 30

People say that honesty is the best policy. Do you agree with that statement? Explain.

Candles come in many different scents. Imagine that you have been asked to select a new candle scent. What would you like this new candle to smell like? Explain.

July 31

Imagine that your pen pal just sent you a huge box in the mail. Write about what happens when you open the box.

Would you rather adopt an animal from a shelter or buy one from a pet store? Explain.

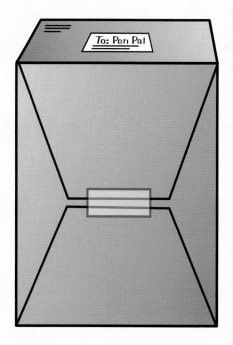

To: Pen Pal

JULY

student

Journal

August

student

Journal

September

Journal

October

Journal

November

Journal

December

Journal

January

Journal

February

student

Journal

March

Journal

April

Journal

May

student

Journal

June

student

Journal

July